THE GREAT FILTER

a play for two astronauts

Frank Winters

BROADWAY PLAY PUBLISHING INC
New York
www.broadwayplaypublishing.com
info@broadwayplaypublishing.com

THE GREAT FILTER
© Copyright 2021 Frank Winters

All rights reserved. This work is fully protected under the copyright laws of the United States of America. No part of this publication may be photocopied, reproduced, stored in a retrieval system, or transmitted, in any form or by any means, electronic, mechanical, recording, or otherwise, without the prior permission of the publisher. Additional copies of this play are available from the publisher.

Written permission is required for live performance of any sort. This includes readings, cuttings, scenes, and excerpts. For amateur and stock performances, please contact Broadway Play Publishing Inc. For all other rights please contact the author c/o B P P I.

First edition: December 2021
I S B N: 978-0-88145-917-3

Book design: Marie Donovan
Page make-up: Adobe InDesign
Typeface: Palatino

The world premiere of THE GREAT FILTER was produced by Scrap Paper Pictures (Producers: Rachel Brosnahan, Paige Simpson & Russell Kahn) and Looks Like A Great Time (Producers: Jason Ralph & Trevor Einhorn) in 2021. The cast and creative contributors were:

DAVID	Jason Ralph
ELI	Trevor Einhorn
Director	Frank Winters
Set design	James Ortiz
Lighting design	Stacey Derosier
Costume design	Max Kaiserman
Stage Manager	Jenny Kennedy
Assistant Stage Manager	Howard Tilkin
Technical Director	David Ralph
Load In T D	Kryssy Wright

Film team:

Co-Producer	Neil Sauvage
Co-Producer	Rachel Walden
Director of Photography	Hunter Zimny
Camera Operator	Connor Shuurmans
1st A C	Eli Freireich
Sound Mixer	Ben Eckersley
D I T / Live Editor	Jordan Schulkin
Camera P A	Vance Johnson
Post House	Resolve Media Group
Equipment Partner	Adorama

CHARACTERS & SETTING

DAVID, *an astronaut*
ELI, *also an astronaut*

While this play was originally written for (and the characters named after) two performers who used he/him/his pronouns, all artists are invited to play these roles and have the author's whole-hearted blessing to change character names and pronouns as you see fit.

This play utilizes the technique wherein the use of a forward slash (/) indicates that it is here that the next line begins in order to achieve an overlapping effect, as pioneered (to the author's understanding) by playwright Caryl Churchill and publisher Nick Hern.

The author would like to acknowledge the works of scientists, artists, and creators including (but certainly not limited to) Enrico Fermi and Frank Drake.

(*As the audience enters the space, they see an isolation chamber; mostly sparse, but for a console used for communications purposes, two beds, a desk, and a digital clock already counting down. As the show begins, the lights fade to black until the darkness is all that's left. Lights up on* DAVID.)

DAVID: Right, so, hi.

(DAVID's *talking to us.* ELI *enters—*)

ELI: Good morning.
(*And speaks to* DAVID)

DAVID: The thing is that I sometimes have a difficult time trying to, um, to talk to people who haven't ever been hunting before.

ELI: How we doin'?

DAVID: And to be clear it isn't that I *love* hunting, but when you're nineteen and your girlfriend's dad puts a rifle in your hands at three-thirty in the morning it isn't really a conversation.

ELI: Feelin' good?

DAVID: And I mention this only because of something that he said, on the way, that it was going to be a lot of *waiting—*

ELI: I slept like shit, actually.

DAVID: Because while this bullet is going to travel around twenty five hundred feet per second, meaning that it can go from the top of the Empire State Building on down to the basement in the same amount of time it takes for you to pull the trigger, it only *works*—if you make that first move.

ELI: Has anyone / been in here today?

DAVID: Because a white-tailed deer is able to hear a twig snap from a quarter of a mile away and then start running up to thirty miles an hour in the time it takes for your weight to shift and so the only way to do it, then, to kill him, he said—

(Beat)

—is to line up your shot, stay very, very still, and then *wait*—for him to come to you, and make sure that by the time he sees the trap, that he's already in it. That he's caught—and it's already over. But *that* isn't even the crazy part because the crazy part, to me, is that if you do it right, if you're patient and if you're quiet enough, if you sit still, and get your placement just right—then he isn't ever even going to hear the sound of the bullet that's going to split his head in two because that little piece of sculpted copper, steel, and nickel will be traveling faster than the speed of it's own *sound* and so the very last thing that he hears—

ELI: Okay.

DAVID: …will be silence.

(Beat)

And that just—

ELI: Are you ready?

(DAVID *hesitates. Turns away from us. And then he turns back.*)

DAVID: Anyway. Um.

(Beat)

Eli hasn't ever been hunting.

(ELI *tosses* DAVID *an outfit for the press conference to start changing into.*)

ELI: Commander Hall, what would you say was the most incredible thing to you about space travel?

DAVID: Well, do you want the real answer or are we just / fuckin' around?

ELI: The real answer.

DAVID: Okay.

ELI: But you know what? Oh. Here's a fun game; you have to work in a specific word into your answer.

DAVID: I like that.

ELI: Right?

DAVID: That's fun.

ELI: I saw a thing about how celebrities / will do that. Okay.

DAVID: I love that. What's my word?

ELI: Marsupial.

DAVID: *(Beat)* I mean, that feels challenging.

ELI: Well, if it wasn't challenging—

DAVID: Okay, you know what I got this, here we go.

ELI: Wait, what's my word?

DAVID: Well, I'm not gonna tell you that now, / that would give you time to prepare.

ELI: No, you're right; you're totally right.

DAVID: I don't even like how much time I've had with this one so before I can even think about it any further okay, the thing that was most incredible to me about space travel, it was like, you spend your whole life dreaming of something just out of reach, of being an *explorer*, you know? When you're a kid and so you spend your whole life looking up, at something way up there, it's like, it's how I imagine a baby marsupial—

ELI: Nice.

DAVID: —thank you when it's still in the pouch must feel seeing those first cracks of light peek in and at that moment when you bridge the gap from here to there you pass through the stratosphere and all of a sudden this place that was *there* for your whole entire life—is now *here*.

(Beat)

And I think that's pretty incredible.

ELI: Can I just say?

DAVID: Yeah?

ELI: Because that was, like.

DAVID: No way that I remember all that.

ELI: I know, but that was art.

DAVID: Okay, your turn.

ELI: We don't need to do me.

DAVID: Why?

ELI: Because I didn't actually / do anything—

DAVID: What are you literally what are the words that you're saying to me right now?

ELI: I stayed on the ship the whole time; nobody—

DAVID: Eli.

ELI: Yeah.

DAVID: Do you know how many people have ever been alive on the planet earth?

ELI: I do not.

DAVID: How many people have ever lived and died on this planet without ever even once going into outer space?

ELI: I feel like you're gonna say a lot. / Is it a lot? It's probably—

DAVID: According to the most recent shaddup the most recent estimate is one hundred and ten billion, which, for some context that's more than one hundred and nine *billion* people who were all born, lived, and died on this planet. Do you know how many of them have ever been to outer space?

ELI: Less than that?

DAVID: Seven hundred and six of which you are now one. That's a hell of a ratio.

ELI: You're right.

DAVID: Now, same question to you only your word, my friend, is "washing machine". / Now, Specialist—

ELI: Okay, that's—two words, but fine.

DAVID: When you were up on the ship—

ELI: Wait, hang on real quick—

DAVID: Yeah bud.

ELI: When was this supposed to start?

DAVID: *(Beat)* In an hour.

ELI: Okay.

DAVID: Right?

ELI: I mean, yes, but daylight's savings time...

DAVID: Right that's—okay, so, but that was what.

ELI: Today.

DAVID: Right.

ELI: So, is it now or is it an hour from now?

DAVID: *(Beat)* I officially have no idea.

ELI: Excellent.

DAVID: You really would have thought that getting back down on the ground would be the hard part.

(ELI *goes to a board of electronic panels, and activates a speaker. As he does this,* DAVID *opens a rucksack and begins packing.*)

ELI: *(Into speaker)* Uh, this is Specialist Elias Wayne, it's—we're just kinda waiting on the press conference to start, but we think there may have been some kind of a mix up with daylight's savings because it's been a while since that was a factor for us, so, if you could offer any clarity as to whether or not the press conference is now or an hour from now or possibly an hour ago, then, that would be great, thank you.

DAVID: Okay.

ELI: *(Into speaker)* Over.

DAVID: You do realize that we're gonna have to change your word now?

ELI: Does this not concern you?

DAVID: That a press conference hasn't started yet? On my list of priorities / that is not particularly high—

ELI: They've just usually contacted us by now, is all I'm saying.

DAVID: Are you freaking out?

ELI: No.

DAVID: Are you sure?

ELI: What's the new word?

DAVID: Okay.
(Beat)
It's marzipan.

ELI: Great.
(Beat)
I do not know what that is.

DAVID: It's like a pastry.

ELI: It's *like* a pastry?

DAVID: It is sugar and honey and almond stuff; Specialist—

ELI: Yes.

DAVID: You've done this astonishing thing, having been a part of a once-in-a-generation experiment that could forever revolutionize the way that humanity interacts with the cosmos—

ELI: Wow.

DAVID: It's how they talk. When you were up there, participating in this unprecedented scientific achievement, what were your thoughts?

ELI: Well, I mean.
(Beat)
Marzipan, / you know?

DAVID: Okay, you know what?

ELI: I don't even know what it is.

DAVID: It is almonds and—

ELI: Well, how about this it was unlike anything I've ever experienced before, not unlike marzipan, / which I have never once in my life experienced.

DAVID: Right because I've got all sorts of history with marsupials. You were the one who wanted to practice.

ELI: Yeah, well, that was before—

DAVID: Before what?

ELI: *(Into speaker)* This is Eli, just—

DAVID: Wow.

ELI: *(Into speaker)* Can I get a five-by-five on this?

DAVID: So, you're choosing *now* to get claustrophobic?

ELI: I'm not, I'm—I just wonder if the communications system isn't fucked. / Maybe.

DAVID: It's working fine.

ELI: Then why isn't anybody responding?

DAVID: Because it's—tech nerds busy dealing with press on a Sunday morning. Relax.

ELI: Can you even see anybody out there?

DAVID: Ask me another question.

ELI: I just did.

DAVID: Okay, you know what? Here.

ELI: Thank you.

DAVID: *(Into speaker)* This is Commander David Hall, can we just get some Xanax in here / for my guy? He's going through a really tough morning, and—

ELI: Okay. Thank you very much. That is really—so glad that's—great.

DAVID: *(Into speaker)* Some coffee would be great but only for me. Thanks.

ELI: Okay.

DAVID: *(Into speaker)* Over.
(To ELI*)*
It's fine. Just—breathe.

ELI: Thank you. What's the next question?

DAVID: Right.

ELI: And what's the new word? Or is there / some new obscure pastry that…?

DAVID: Well, what about the other—more difficult questions?

ELI: What do you mean?

DAVID: *(Beat)* Nothing.

ELI: No, / what do you mean?

DAVID: I'll take care of it.

ELI: I'm serious / there's been a number of—

DAVID: You were talking about proposing to Sam? Or no you were thinking about it?

ELI: I am, yeah.

DAVID: Thinking about it?

ELI: Yes.

DAVID: Well, don't.

ELI: I'm sorry?

DAVID: You should just do it.

ELI: I see.

DAVID: Pull the trigger. You find the right person and is Sammy the right person?

ELI: Yes.

DAVID: Then don't even think about it; you find that person and it's basically like nothing changed except there's this weight off, now. You have a fight and okay, well, we're gonna figure it out. It's terrifying, but you do it together. You made a *vow*. The whole thing, it's— highly recommended.

ELI: Have you ever been married?

DAVID: No. But I hear wonderful things.

ELI: Okay. Well, I will take that under advisement.

DAVID: Good.

ELI: You know, I was thinking that—if you wanted, when all this is over, the inquest and, whatever, Sammy's parents live out by this lake, it's beautiful, at night, you can look up, and—anyway, I thought that maybe, if you wanted, we could go, and—

DAVID: That sounds great.

ELI: Really?

DAVID: Yeah, I'd love that.

ELI: Good, no, yeah, because actually, I thought—

DAVID: That I was talking about the other stuff?

ELI: A little bit. Yeah.

DAVID: Well, you don't have to worry about that.

ELI: I'm just saying that if they do bring it up—

DAVID: Which, they will.

ELI: Right.

DAVID: I mean, of course they will.

ELI: So, then I could field that one. Um. If you wanted—

DAVID: I mean, we have the written statement, it's a little impersonal, but otherwise.

ELI: I know, I just—

DAVID: It felt to me like they weren't all that interested in any deviation from that, so.

ELI: I just wanted to offer—

DAVID: And I appreciate that, but—

ELI: What?

DAVID: Well.
(Beat)
You weren't there. Right?

ELI: Sure.

DAVID: I mean you weren't on the secondary craft.

ELI: I was *on* the mission.

DAVID: This isn't personal.

ELI: I know that.

DAVID: It just feels like my responsibility, we've got a written statement which I will read and then we go home.

ELI: Great.

(*Into speaker*)

Listen, could I just get the Cubs score, whatever? Any confirmation that all communications systems are operational, please, would be great. Over.

DAVID: Are you freaking out?

ELI: No.

DAVID: A little bit?

ELI: You want to come take a look at this?

DAVID: Sure.

ELI: Thank you.

(DAVID *runs some diagnostics on the main control panel.*)

ELI: Is that true, that, what you said before, that, as a kid that you wanted to be an *explorer*?

DAVID: It sure is.

ELI: Of course you did.

DAVID: That or a pharmacist.

ELI: Well, it's always one of the two.

DAVID: Relays are all solid. It might be the input transducer but that's not something I can tell for sure without causing some minor damage.

ELI: Well, what kinda damage / are we talking about?

DAVID: About two hundred and fifty.

ELI: Thousand?

DAVID: Yeah.

ELI: Dollars?

DAVID: Yeah.

ELI: Talk to me about marzipan.

(But DAVID keeps digging until—)

DAVID: Hang on.

ELI: What?

DAVID: I'm getting noise.

ELI: Is it satellite?

DAVID: No, it's—

ELI: What?

DAVID: I think it's *radio*.

ELI: *(Beat)* Really.

DAVID: Yeah.

ELI: Is it *Car Talk*?

DAVID: Hang on.

ELI: Because I love those guys.

DAVID: Just gimme one second.
(He grabs a small, metallic object and uses it to wrench open a panel. He starts fiddling with some wires—)

ELI: You know, her family has this card game, right, and, every time that we play it I'm, like, ninety percent sure that she changes the rules in these very subtle but important ways they have this look that they give each other and I know I sound paranoid but / if you're there—

DAVID: Sorry, can you just—hand me that? Right over there?

ELI: Yeah.

DAVID: Thanks.

ELI: Um. Are we supposed to be doing—this? Whatever it is that—you're doing?

DAVID: Well, that is a very interesting question there, Eli.

ELI: I'm serious.
(He snaps part of the intercom in half and plugs part of it into a makeshift headphone—)

DAVID: Me too, it is a very…interesting…

(Something's weird.)

ELI: What?

DAVID: Hang on.

ELI: What is it?

DAVID: Just—
(Beat)
Um. Do you have a—?

ELI: Yeah. Sure.

(ELI hands DAVID the press release and a pencil.)

DAVID: Thanks.

ELI: What is it?

(DAVID writes on the back of the press release. He listens. He writes it again. Something's up.)

DAVID: Um.
(He listens again.)

ELI: Everything okay?

DAVID: Yeah.

ELI: May I?

DAVID: Please.

(ELI crawls under the panel and starts listening.)

ELI: Okay. What am I listening to?

DAVID: You don't hear that?

ELI: No, I hear—something. / It's—static, mostly.

DAVID: Right no wait for it to; see, it's repeating. Listen now. To that. Now.

ELI: *(Listening)* Okay.

DAVID: Do you hear that?

ELI: Wait, hang on.

DAVID: Dah-dih, dah-dah-dah.

ELI: I mean—/ I can hear *something*.

DAVID: Dah-dah-dah…

ELI: I just—it's really / hard to make out—

DAVID: Dah-dah-dah, / dih-dih-dah, dih-dah-dih, dah-dah-dah-dih…

ELI: In, what—that would be—Morse Code? Right?

DAVID: Yeah. It's the same thing repeating over / and over again—

ELI: Saying what? What is it saying?

(And DAVID *moves to the communications panel.)*

DAVID: *(Into speaker)* Um. This is Commander Hall requesting confirmation of message receipt please, over.

ELI: Is everything okay?

(Beat)

DAVID: *(Into speaker)* This is Commander David Hall requesting immediate confirmation of message receipt please fucking now, over. Do you copy?

ELI: Hey.

DAVID: *(Into speaker)* Clearance code alpha, um. Or. Fuck.

ELI: Hang on.

DAVID: *(Into speaker)* Alpha seven Juliet one seven tango I swear to Christ I need an answer from somebody right fucking now, okay? CQD / this is not a fucking joke.

ELI: All right, maybe we should—

DAVID: *(Into speaker)* Can you hear us.

ELI: David.

DAVID: *What.*

ELI: *(Beat—gently)* Sorry. What did the, um. Transmission—say?

DAVID: *(Beat)* Nothing.

ELI: C'mon.

DAVID: I mean, it was probably / nothing.

ELI: Meaning what?

DAVID: That I probably just, I thought I heard something, and -

ELI: Well, the last time that you thought you heard something—

DAVID: Eli.

ELI: —that was probably nothing? You saved my life. So.
(Beat)
What did it say?

DAVID: It just doesn't make any sense.

ELI: What doesn't?

DAVID: The message.

ELI: Well, what is it?

DAVID: Um.
(Beat)
"No survivors."
(Beat)
It said *"no survivors."*

ELI: Really?

DAVID: Yes.

ELI: In Morse Code?

DAVID: Which, for the record, I haven't done since Boy Scouts—

ELI: But you are sure of what it said?

DAVID: Yes.

ELI: "No survivors."

DAVID: Yeah.

ELI: And that was the *whole* message?

DAVID: It was just repeating / over and over.

ELI: But it wasn't like…a part of a message, it was the whole thing?

DAVID: Yes.

ELI: And that isn't like, a *military*…thing?

DAVID: No.

ELI: Okay. Well, they weren't talking about us.

DAVID: Right.

ELI: Obviously. So, what does that mean, then?

DAVID: You wanna get the fuck out of here?

ELI: *(Beat)* Well, wait, what do you think it means?

DAVID: *It means that I don't know it wasn't about us.* So, I would like to get the fuck out. Okay?

ELI: I mean—yeah.

DAVID: Good.

ELI: But—how?

DAVID: *(Beat)* I'm working on that.

ELI: Okay, well, what frequency is it broadcasting on?

DAVID: It's on all of them.

ELI: Are you sure?

DAVID: No.

ELI: Can you be sure? Maybe?

DAVID: Yeah.

ELI: Sorry. Just if there's any other information...

(DAVID *heads back into the intestines of the communications set-up.*)

DAVID: No, you're right.

ELI: I mean, not to point out the obvious, but there *were*...survivors.

DAVID: Right.

ELI: You and I, we—did that.

DAVID: Yeah.

ELI: So, is it possible that we're just intercepting a message that—

DAVID: No. / And yes, it's on every frequency.

ELI: So, what in the fuck are they talking about?
(*He jumps up and down—waves his arms.*)
HELLO?! Can anyone—

(*As* DAVID *continues looking.*)

ELI: I can't see—anybody. Do you see anything?

DAVID: No.

ELI: So, what is going on?

DAVID: I, um.
(*Beat*)
I really don't know.

(*And for* DAVID, *something has changed. And* ELI *can see, for the first time, that* DAVID *looks genuinely concerned.*)

(DAVID *takes a long, hard look at the clock, counting down—and begins to move, assessing the space around him with focus and new purpose.*)

ELI: Well, I mean. It's probably nothing. Right? They were probably just—

(Beat)

Um.

(Beat)

Out of curiosity, how thick are these windows?

DAVID: You ever try and kick an airplane door open?

ELI: No.

DAVID: I mean, while it was in the air?

ELI: You're saying this would be harder?

DAVID: I am.

ELI: Okay. Well, could we get a message *out*? To someone, maybe?

DAVID: I mean, even if there *weren't* a very impressive firewall that message is still jamming every goddam frequency, / over and over again.

ELI: Can we trace a signal source, then? See if we can't—

DAVID: I can trace a thousand of them. Which is the problem. They all lead to the same place.

ELI: Read it to me again. / In the code, we can—

DAVID: You already know what it says.

ELI: Okay, but that doesn't mean / that there isn't something else we could…

DAVID: *Reading it again isn't.* Here. You want to listen to it again? Fine.

ELI: I couldn't hear it the first time / and even if I did you said it was Morse Code?

DAVID: Wait, you couldn't hear it or you couldn't understand it?

ELI: Well.

DAVID: No, Eli, you couldn't *hear* it—or you couldn't understand it?

ELI: *(Beat)* Look. Whatever it is, I'm sure it's fine.

DAVID: Really.

ELI: Yes.

DAVID: Why?

ELI: Because at least one of us needs to stay calm, and—

DAVID: I am calm I'm thinking about all of the different things I'd need to break in order to get the fuck out of here.

ELI: I thought you said it would be like kicking an airplane door open.

DAVID: Which is why "kicking" is not on my list.

ELI: Okay, so, what other options are there?

DAVID: Um.

ELI: Could we take—

DAVID: It's a closed system with a vacuum seal if we could somehow redirect the pressure from one of the back up generators into a J-cell unit with enough force then, we could theoretically use that same pressure to force open the causeway, or else. Possibly.

ELI: Explode.

DAVID: Yeah.

ELI: Okay. So, there isn't *actually* any other way. You can just say that.

DAVID: Well, I didn't say that.

ELI: Do you think that, maybe they found something?

DAVID: What do you mean?

ELI: There is a *reason* why we're in here.

DAVID: We've been in here for three weeks.

ELI: And we were working with some pretty potent materials up there and…I dunno, maybe they found something.

DAVID: I've had twenty-one clean bills of health already. If they were going to find anything—

ELI: But if the incubation period of—

DAVID: What?

ELI: Whatever is longer than that.

DAVID: Then you come in here and run an X-ray, C T, C B C, fluoroscopic dosimeter or you get a frikkin you get a Geiger counter in here but you do not just cut off communication like this. You do not just start tapping out "no survivors" like the Titanic is sinking.

ELI: I mean, you *seem* calm.

DAVID: And you said *one* of us. Hold this, please.

ELI: Should I just put this / on your tab?

DAVID: Hang on.
(He jumps up; pulls himself up, and is now crawling in the ceiling, checking things.)

ELI: What are you—

DAVID: Fuck.

(The lights flicker.)

ELI: Are you okay?

DAVID: Mildly electrocuted / but it's fine.

ELI: Excuse me?

DAVID: One second.

ELI: Would you come down from there, please?

DAVID: Just one second.

ELI: Yeah. Fine.
(Beat)
Also, the Titanic *had* survivors.

DAVID: Shit.

ELI: What is it?
(He climbs back down.)

DAVID: Sensors on the P R D all look normal and there haven't been any changes since the last time we checked exposure.

ELI: So, you're saying it *isn't* radiation poisoning?

DAVID: I'm saying if it wasn't before, it isn't now only *now* I am starting to get pissed off.

ELI: Why?

DAVID: *Because this doesn't make any sense.* They are twenty-five yards away if the communications system *were* busted, which it's not, they could just walk over here and replace the entire apparatus with two cans and a string. We've got two monitors / on a twelve-hour rotation—

ELI: But, like you said. Maybe they're busy.

DAVID: For this long? No, it's—if they aren't responding by now it's because they either *can't*, which, doesn't make any sense—

ELI: Right.

DAVID: —or they won't.
(Beat)
Which maybe does.

(And a penny drops.)

ELI: What do you mean, that—they won't? Why *wouldn't* they?
(*Beat*)
David.
(*He looks terrified.*)
DAVID: Yeah.

ELI: What does that mean?

DAVID: You know what? Don't worry about it.

ELI: Excuse me?

DAVID: I'll be right back.
(*He makes his way back up into the ceiling.*)

ELI: No hang on, is there—do you know something that I don't?

DAVID: There isn't really a nice way for me to answer that.

ELI: Where are you going?

DAVID: I'll be right back.
(*And he's gone.*)

ELI: Okay, I think that, maybe we're getting a little bit ahead of ourselves here, so, why don't we take some nice, deep breaths?

DAVID: I wouldn't recommend that.

(*The lights flicker.*)

ELI: Wait, why? Are we—hang on, are we running low on oxygen?

DAVID: We are running *low* on information so until we know for sure what we have and for how long we'll need it—

ELI: Then let's work the problem.

DAVID: Yes.

ELI: Start with what we do know. Build out from there.

DAVID: Great.

ELI: Good.

DAVID: And now that we've exhausted that option.

ELI: I'm serious. We start from the top. It was a mission to test out the phase two matching capabilities for the TF-7 cloud seeding, right? We were successful in… some, if not *all* primary mission objectives, and not without…um. We returned to earth and spent three weeks in Isolation Protocol; there is supposed to be a press conference only what in the fuck / are you doing up there.

DAVID: I'm just looking around.

ELI: You're freaking me out.

DAVID: Take deep breaths.

ELI: I thought I wasn't supposed to.

DAVID: You're right, do not take deep breaths. Just keep going.

(The lights flicker again. DAVID *is definitely doing something. And now* ELI's *getting frustrated, too.)*

ELI: Okay. Um, is there any chance that it's a code?

DAVID: The transmission?

ELI: Yeah.

DAVID: No.

ELI: Why.

DAVID: Because it was already in code.

ELI: Right.

DAVID: It was *Morse* code. / But forget about the transmission.

ELI: But beyond that—I mean, is it—could it be an anagram?

DAVID: "On Survivors."

ELI: Or maybe "vivo" something, "vivo soon"? Is that anything?

DAVID: You're right; I feel so empowered / by this knowledge. Forget about the transmission.

ELI: You know, you can go electrocute yourself again, really, any time you like.

DAVID: Okay.

ELI: What other kinds of codes are there? It could be a cypher?

DAVID: It isn't a code. / And it isn't a cypher.

ELI: Well, how do you know that?

DAVID: Because the Zodiac Killer isn't running this mission.

ELI: And it isn't World War One so you explain to me how come we're getting Morse Code on a radio frequency.
(Beat)
Right?
(Beat)
David.

DAVID: Yeah?

ELI: Are you okay up there?

DAVID: *(Beat)* Um. Yeah, I just um.

ELI: What?

DAVID: I kinda—found something.

ELI: What do you mean? What did you find?

DAVID: I'm gonna come back down—

ELI: Okay.

DAVID: —but I do not want you to freak out.

ELI: *(Beat)* Okay?

DAVID: I'm coming back down.

ELI: All right but why would the *fuck is that?*

(DAVID *has a small handgun.*)

DAVID: Be calm.

ELI: What is that?

DAVID: It's a semiautomatic M9.

ELI: Which—you said you *found* that?

DAVID: Yeah.

ELI: Up in the—

DAVID: Yeah.

ELI: Do they usually have—those inside of the ceiling?

DAVID: No.

ELI: So, what in the fuck—

DAVID: I do not know. But remember you asked how we get out of here?

ELI: Yeah.

DAVID: Take a step back for me, would you?

ELI: Hang on.

DAVID: Pressurization puts us at, what?

ELI: David, I am gonna ask you to please put the gun down.

DAVID: Why?

ELI: Because you're scaring the shit out of me.

DAVID: You'd rather wait until we run out of oxygen?

ELI: Why would we be running out of oxygen?

DAVID: You don't feel a little bit light headed?

ELI: That's because you're hyperventilating, / which by the way—

DAVID: I'm not. I'm asking you.

ELI: I feel fine.

DAVID: Really?

ELI: Aside from you scaring the crap out of me? Yes. I feel great.

DAVID: Well, I don't.

ELI: Would you put the gun down, please?

DAVID: Ya know, I would, but somebody keeps on repeating "NO SURVIVORS" / over and over again in Morse Code and so just on principle, I would like to get out of here.

ELI: And we are going to figure out what's going on with that, the transmission, all of it but I don't think shooting holes in the wall is gonna solve anything.

DAVID: I am *aiming*—for the window.

ELI: And what if this is a lockdown?

DAVID: *(Beat)* What do you mean?

ELI: I mean, that transmission could be a *warning*, okay? Because out there, they are *also* working with some pretty potent materials and you said the transmission read "No Survivors"? Well, what if it isn't—"no survivors" in here, it's—

DAVID: Do you really believe / that's what's happening?

ELI: Would you just, would you put. The gun. Down. Please.

(Beat. DAVID lowers the gun.)

ELI: No, like. Would you—over there, maybe? Please.

(DAVID puts the gun down. On the table)

ELI: Thanks. Thank you very much. For that.

(So. There is now a gun on the table.)

DAVID: So you think this is a lockdown?

ELI: I don't know.

DAVID: Evacuation, whatever?

ELI: I have no idea, but it would check a lot of boxes. Right? If there were some kind of an emergency then that's why nobody's—

(DAVID checks the communications system again.)

ELI: Anything?

DAVID: No.

ELI: If everybody had to get the fuck out, then. Right?

DAVID: *(Beat)* Maybe.

ELI: Okay, so, let's call that Option A. Right? No, this is good.

(He grabs the pencil and piece of paper and begins making a new list.)

That there was some kind of an event, whatever. Outside of our isolation zone which prompted emergency evac let's say very suddenly; they left us in here, why, because they knew the pressurization would keep us somehow, what?

DAVID: Secluded.

ELI: *Protected* from the event which also suggests that it can be prevented by—

DAVID: Which does not explain either the gun or the transmission.

ELI: We're taking it one step at a time.

DAVID: Which we do not have time for; and "No Survivors" does not exactly—

ELI: What?

DAVID: Inspire all that much confidence; and we can last up to four minutes in here without oxygen under the very best of circumstances, which this is not.

ELI: Well, we have plenty of oxygen—

DAVID: Great. We *also* used to have plenty of communication with our friends over there and now we don't.

ELI: So, you think that—

DAVID: Bad things can happen very quickly? Yes. / Historically? Fucking yes.

ELI: But that's—what I'm saying is do you really think that—

DAVID: What?
(And it dawns on him that he does.)

ELI: Or do you honestly *believe* that—

DAVID: Yeah?
(Beat)
No, say it.

ELI: That they're trying to kill us?

DAVID: And we're on to Option B.

(DAVID snatches the list from ELI's hand.)

ELI: Are you serious right now?

DAVID: Well, you were the one who said, didn't you say that maybe they found something?

ELI: Okay fine but, these are people that we know. That we work with. These are good people.

DAVID: I know, maybe one of them gave us a gun.

ELI: I'm serious.

DAVID: So am I.

ELI: But. I mean, there are faster ways of, even...*if* they wanted to kill us, they could just turn off the oxygen, right?

DAVID: They *haven't*; doesn't mean that they won't. In fact it doesn't even mean that they haven't; and *you* were feeling light-headed.

ELI: That was you.

DAVID: Right.

ELI: Look, just for the sake of argument, they have been coming in here every day for three weeks with food, water, running labs / and drawing blood, if they wanted to kill us—

DAVID: Which they haven't today and you won't even *consider* this as option B?

ELI: *(Beat)* What's option C?

DAVID: Thank you. So, Option C—

(ELI *turns out and speaks to us as* DAVID *continues with the list, furiously.*)

ELI: In nineteen fifty there was, hi, a group of scientists having lunch, they were astrophysicists and nuclear engineers and everybody was talking about how given the fact that there are billions of stars in our galaxy and the law of large numbers would indicate that at least some of them would have the ability of supporting life on a planet not unlike the one that we live on, if all of these things are true, at the same time, then it would also stand to reason that life, of some kind, would evolve in a way not dissimilar from our own and that's not even considering that space extends out indefinitely and therefore only increases exponentially the statistical possibilities when a guy named Enrico Fermi, he smashes his hand down on the table, and says, "Okay, so, where the fuck is everybody?"

DAVID: Option G.

ELI: Only possibly he said that in Italian?

DAVID: H.

ELI: And I have no idea if he cursed, when he said that. But this is called the Fermi Paradox:

DAVID: I.

ELI: If it is by an almost laughably enormous margin of probability that we are not alone in the universe, then—

DAVID: K.

ELI: Where the fuck is everybody?

DAVID: Oh, okay, and also.

ELI: And so with apologies to Frank Drake there are an awful lot of really good potential solutions to this problem and I'm gonna tell you my three favorite ones, the first being Zoo Theory—

DAVID: L.

ELI: Which would be an excellent band name and stipulates that there may be, in fact, a whole great big bustling hypothetical intergalactic civilization out there, *Star Trek*, basically, with planets and starships and space stations, but that they consider us to be something like koala bears and have us roped off the from the rest of the universe for our own safety until we can properly tie our own shoelaces.

DAVID: O.

ELI: Then there's the idea that just by happenstance, that we are the first ones at the party, because just technically speaking, *somebody* has to be and why not us, the theory that we just so happen to be the first species to get to a point in our own evolution where we're sending out radio-waves and even attempting interstellar travel and so it's not that nobody's *listening*—it's just that nobody else has figured out how to pick up what we're putting down, which is, I think, ultimately... quite hopeful.

DAVID: R...

ELI: But you cannot have that theory without acknowledging the very real possibility of the much more depressing opposite, bringing us to the odds-on Vegas favorite being the Great Filter.

DAVID: T...

ELI: A sort of nihilistic Neo-Malthusian buzzkill of an idea that I happen to find extremely compelling because of—

DAVID: U...

ELI: Well...

DAVID: V...

ELI: Everything.

DAVID: X...

ELI: That there is a natural sort of weeding-out-point ceiling for advanced civilizations like ours, that when you consider the fact that in the scheme of things it took us about five minutes to go from inventing the means by which we generate fire to the means by which we generate nuclear holocaust...

DAVID: Y...

ELI: That species just do not make it past a certain point, a kind of say-it-with-me-now, Great Filter, that every civilization is doomed to the same bloody and irradiated destiny: if we can create the technologies required to allow us to do these great and beautiful things like travel the fucking stars then we will just inexorably use those same technologies...

DAVID: And…

ELI: …to destroy ourselves first.
(Beat)
Although, just me personally?
(Beat)
Looking up at a sky that we know to be endlessly vast and, armed only with the absolute certainty that we have mapped less than five percent of it, of *our* known universe, I just.
(Beat)
I dunno. Me personally?

DAVID: Okay, so—

ELI: I don't think we're done looking.

DAVID: We are gonna need a bigger alphabet.

(DAVID *firmly places the paper into* ELI's *hand before earnestly getting to work.*)

ELI: Where are you going?

DAVID: Don't worry about it.

(DAVID *begins ripping wires out of the wall, etc.* ELI *looks down at the page—*)

ELI: Okay, but—just.
(Beat—reads)
Hang on. David?
(And is suddenly concerned)

DAVID: Yeah.

ELI: What is this?

DAVID: It is a non-exhaustive list / of all possibilities that—

ELI: Worst case scenarios?

DAVID: Exactly.

ELI: Okay and so you think that all of this is…a dream? Or that.

DAVID: Listen.

ELI: Space-time is / closing in on itself?

DAVID: I think it's possible; I didn't say it was probable, look—

ELI: Does this say robots?

DAVID: We are coming to the scary part, here.
(Beat)
Because the problem isn't mechanical. There isn't anything wrong with the input transducer or the rotary; there isn't any reason why they shouldn't be able to talk to us from a technological perspective which means the problem is with the people.

ELI: What does that mean?

DAVID: This isn't going to be like last time; I can't protect you from everything, but there is something I need you to do for me.

ELI: Yeah?

DAVID: The further we go, the more your brain is gonna want to find reasons not to trust me and I'm just—I'm gonna ask you to challenge that as much as you can, all right?

ELI: Okay, but.

DAVID: Good. Thank you.
(He takes the small makeshift metal object and pries open another panel.)

ELI: So. Of all of these you still think that…that Option B.

DAVID: Yeah.

ELI: Okay and just…but *why* would they be all of a sudden / trying to kill us?

DAVID: Which is assuming it's all of a sudden.

ELI: But is that actually what you think is going on here?

DAVID: *(Beat)* I don't know.

ELI: So then maybe we should stop ripping things out of the walls, and—

DAVID: But you said 'work the problem', right?

ELI: I sure did, yeah.

DAVID: Well, here's my problem I was over two hundred million miles away on a spacecraft that was mostly on fire and I didn't lose communication with anyone in this building where there are / generators and back up generators—

ELI: And so what are you doing?

DAVID: I'm working the fucking problem.

(DAVID *makes an adjustment—the lights flicker. In fact, one of the lights goes out. Making the room a little darker)*

ELI: And you think the broadcast—

DAVID: It isn't about the transmission it's about our mission was a fucking calamity, and—

ELI: It wasn't a *calamity*.

DAVID: Excuse me?

ELI: *(Beat)* What?

DAVID: No, what did you just say?

ELI: Look.

DAVID: You weren't there.

ELI: I was there.

DAVID: No, you were on the primary; three people died. On the secondary craft but you weren't there for that.

ELI: I meant in terms of—

DAVID: No, I know what you *meant* but you didn't see that. Them. You weren't there. For that.
(Beat)
And we are running out of time.
(He dumps his shit out of the bag he was packing earlier; starts putting his supplies inside as he digs more deeply into the wall.)

ELI: What are you talking about?

(The lights flicker again.)

DAVID: The very literal countdown clock that is / sitting right over there—

ELI: A publicity thing counting down to us leaving the isolation deck and, right?

DAVID: Sure.

ELI: Heading down to the press conference which *could* still happen.

DAVID: Because astrophysicists tend to become *stymied* by daylight's savings time?

ELI: So, you're saying that the clock, it means what?

DAVID: No idea. But if you wanted to keep two people in one place for—whatever reason without asking any questions—look at me—isn't this *exactly* what you would do?

ELI: I really haven't thought about it.

DAVID: Well, fucking think about it, okay?

ELI: David.

DAVID: Get back to me.
(He climbs back up with the rucksack and gets to work.)

ELI: How long have you been thinking about this?

DAVID: Don't worry about that.

(He begins tearing more shit out of the wall, then moves to a new area.)

ELI: And what is this one? I think it says "damage control"? / Option O.

DAVID: Right.

ELI: What does that mean?

DAVID: Gimme one second, okay?

(The lights flicker again—another goes out.)

ELI: Seriously, what are you doing up there?

DAVID: I'm building a bomb.

ELI: *(Beat)* Okay, you know what? Let's start over—

DAVID: Remember what I said?

ELI: Yes.

DAVID: Good, because *something* isn't right here, and that clock is counting down *to something* ergo—

ELI: You're building a—a bomb?

DAVID: Yes.

ELI: But, like an actual—

DAVID: Yes.

ELI: This is, like. I really can't tell if you're joking.

DAVID: I'm not.

ELI: Okay. And…but what are you building this… *bomb*…out of?

DAVID: I mean, the wall.

ELI: Right.

DAVID: Stuff inside of the wall.

ELI: I honestly—I really can't tell if you're kidding. Or not.

DAVID: Eli?

ELI: Yeah.

DAVID: I'm really not.

ELI: *(Beat)* Okay, but. Yes, you are.

DAVID: So, then why did you ask?

ELI: Because yes you fucking are, this is—not—that—no.

DAVID: Okay.

(ELI *crosses to the COMMS panel. Still nothing. The lights flicker again—and another one goes out. Fuck)*

ELI: And what is "Damage Control"? It's—you have a thing next to it.

(DAVID *picks up the press conference packet, flips to a page and reads.)*

DAVID: Okay.
(Reading)
"The TF-7 Cloud Seeding remains an integral part of and crowning achievement in our terraformation initiative" except that it fucking wasn't; the TF-7 did not match, does not work; the sequence overloaded and three people, because they were on the wrong side of a door, just.
(Beat)
There wasn't ever going to be a press conference. For this. Us. This whole thing was a fucking calamity. So.
(Beat)
"Damage control." Okay?
(Beat)
Meaning you were right.

ELI: How so?

DAVID: "No Survivors" *was*, probably, a code.
(Into speaker)
Ah, hi, there.

ELI: What are you doing?

DAVID: *(Into speaker)* This is Commander David Hall, and what I'm doing right now is building a bomb which will have a blast radius of at the very least this entire building and so here's what happens next—I have created a kind of R F I D fail-safe which should remain open for you to make contact if for some reason, you cannot utilize any other method of communication, however—if that door doesn't open or contact isn't established by the time that clock reaches, oh, let's say ten seconds, I am going to detonate this bomb which I have no desire to do but I think we can all agree that I fucking will.
(Beat)
So. We look forward to hearing from you. Over and out.

(And he heads back to work.)

ELI: Is this serious?

DAVID: Yeah.

ELI: You're building / a bomb?

DAVID: We've been over this.

ELI: Okay, but there could be innocent people out there / and—

DAVID: Really?

ELI: Yeah.

DAVID: Then why are they letting us *rot* in here? / These very good people—

ELI: It's been a half an hour; we don't even know yet—

DAVID: So, what's your time-table, then? We could be out of oxygen any second and that clock—

ELI: Could be meaningless. And by the way there are innocent people in here. Hi.

DAVID: Hi. Look, I don't want to detonate this bomb; I also didn't want to have a press conference. I wanted to walk out of here and sleep in a bed with sheets that weren't made of aluminum foil, but if that isn't going to happen—

ELI: Slow down.

DAVID: And that *isn't* going to happen—

ELI: I think we should just wait, though. Right? Doesn't that sound like / the most reasonable thing—

DAVID: In any other situation?

ELI: —is to just wait and see what happens when the clock runs out?

DAVID: Fucking—no.
(He pries open a third panel—)

ELI: Why?

DAVID: *Because that is what they are doing.* Right now. They are waiting for the perfect moment which by the way is getting closer; what about this do you not get? We were supposed to change the world.
(Beat)
And we didn't.
(Beat)
People have disappeared. And been disappeared for a lot less. I know these people. It's how their minds work, so, no, I don't think that we should wait. Because when that clock runs out I don't think that we will ever be able to do anything; not ever again, so. No.

(Beat)

ELI: Okay, look, I get that all of this is happening very quickly and after what you've been through, / I can't blame you for feeling like—

DAVID: And on the list, I already have that one of us has gone crazy so—

ELI: I didn't say "crazy", it's—you have experienced a very severe trauma.

DAVID: And you haven't?

ELI: It's different.

DAVID: Why?

ELI: Because I wasn't—

DAVID: I see.

ELI: I was on the primary, / like you said. I didn't—

DAVID: No, what you mean to say is that you didn't have to push the fucking button. Right?

ELI: *(Beat)* What I meant to say is—

DAVID: Yeah?

ELI: That I am going to need your help / if we are going to get through this—

DAVID: Well, what do you think I'm doing?

ELI: *Building a fucking bomb.*
(Beat)
Because you're scared. But it isn't going to fix this problem.

DAVID: Eli, sitting quietly on our hands? Isn't going to fix this problem, either.

ELI: I'm not saying that we should / sit on our hands.

DAVID: If there are people out there watching us then they aren't gonna let us destroy ourselves, their tech, and them, in the process. I am just…forcing *their* hand.

ELI: And if there aren't people out there?

DAVID: Then we're *fucked*; only I don't think that's gonna happen; I think there are people out there right now, they are watching us—

ELI: Based on what?

DAVID: Well, do you hear that?

ELI: Hear what?

DAVID: No, I mean, really, just—listen.

ELI: I don't—

DAVID: Hang on. Just. Listen.
(Beat)
No sirens, no alarms. No flashing lights or pre-recorded audio. We have no supplies, no communication with the outside world, and, increasingly, no time. They haven't had to quarantine astronauts like this since the sixties, so what does all this sound like? To you?

ELI: *(Beat)* I don't know.

DAVID: Exactly. Because they control what we know. / The oxygen that we breathe?

ELI: But we knew that there were going to be enhanced protocols—

(DAVID *shoves an official manual into* ELI's *hands.*)

DAVID: Read this—cover to cover, because I have—and there are rules and regulations for everything, protocols to follow in the event of a snow storm in Florida but a communications blackout? Like this? A message? Like that? Is nowhere.

ELI: So you're saying, what, is happening?

DAVID: *I've got no idea;* but before that clock runs out, they will *fold,* and make their presence known.

ELI: And if they don't?

DAVID: Then we will make *our* presence known but it will happen on our terms.
(He goes back to the panel and starts fucking with it again.)

ELI: And the clock?

(He stops.)

DAVID: Oh.

(Beat)

I mean, I dunno, it's NASA. They love a countdown.

(And DAVID pulls out what he needs. The lights flicker again until more lights go out. Getting pretty dark in here)

ELI: Well, they're cutting it pretty close / if they are out there—

DAVID: No, right now they are running around, checking medical histories and mental health records, trying to figure out if I'm bluffing or not.

ELI: Okay, well, I'm gonna let you know right now that *that* isn't going to happen.

(And DAVID stops.)

DAVID: Okay.

ELI: You are not going to detonate a bomb / in this room.

DAVID: Oh really?

ELI: Because you don't want to detonate a bomb in this room.

DAVID: No, I really don't but since when / does that mean that—

ELI: No, I know you and you are not about to kill a bunch of people because they went off COMMS / for a half hour.

DAVID: You don't know that—

ELI: What?

DAVID: *(Beat)* We don't know that it's a half hour.

ELI: What are you talking about?

DAVID: Have you heard from them this morning? From anyone?

ELI: No.

DAVID: Yeah, me neither. In fact, for all we know it's been over fifteen hours since we heard anything from anyone and not for nothing but they didn't do any external maintenance on the first or third / filtration systems—

ELI: When?

DAVID: I'm sorry?

ELI: When did they not do maintenance / that they were supposed to do—

DAVID: Okay, you remember the thing that I said?

ELI: Did you not sleep last night?

DAVID: I said your brain would / start finding reasons—

ELI: How long have you not been sleeping?

DAVID: That doesn't matter.

ELI: Why does that not matter?

DAVID: Because they are going to fold.

ELI: And if they don't?

DAVID: If they are watching us go through this and they don't care—

ELI: I don't care.

DAVID: *Then it isn't on me what happens next.*

ELI: *(Beat)* I mean, yeah but.

DAVID: What?

ELI: I just. We are scientists, we do not just blow shit up.

DAVID: Eli? We are employees of the U S government. Blowing shit up is exactly what we do.

ELI: And that's why *we* deserve to die?

DAVID: Oh, fuck off.

ELI: Or *you* deserve to die? Is this, like?

DAVID: What.

ELI: Did something happen up there? That, maybe I don't know about?

DAVID: I really don't have time / for this right now.

ELI: On the secondary craft? Is there something you didn't tell me?

DAVID: I told you everything that you needed to know.

ELI: That isn't an answer.

(Another light goes out.)

DAVID: I told you what happened; the press department told you what happened up there—

ELI: You said you didn't like the press statement.

DAVID: I said it was "impersonal" I didn't say it wasn't true.

ELI: Is it true?

DAVID: No.

(DAVID tosses ELI a flashlight and heads back up to the crawlspace. ELI crosses to the desk where he picks up the written statement.)

ELI: *(Reading)* "We are deeply saddened by the tragic and unavoidable loss of life which occurred during this mission—our hearts go out to the families of" which part of that isn't true?

DAVID: Well, first of all?

ELI: Yeah.

DAVID: Nobody uses the word 'saddened' in real life. How are you? Oh, me, I'm *saddened*.

ELI: Are you done?

DAVID: Very nearly.

ELI: What happened on the secondary craft?

DAVID: It wasn't unavoidable.
(Beat)
Okay? Is what isn't true. Are you happy? / Am I cured now?

ELI: What does that mean?

DAVID: Holy crap.

ELI: What?

DAVID: I *am* cured now.

ELI: David.

DAVID: No, really, you did it. You got me to say the thing and now I'm cured.

ELI: No, what do you mean / that it wasn't unavoidable? You ran out of time, is that—that's how come it was your fault?

DAVID: If I put a quarter in do you play other songs?

ELI: That's the reason because you had to close the cascade door? Is that it?

DAVID: I will give you a shiny new nickel / if you just shut the fuck up.

ELI: The room was flooded; by closing that door, no listen to me, you saved the TF-7 which is still the best chance that we have and by the way you also saved my fucking life but the accident / was not your fault.

DAVID: Oh my fucking god.

ELI: It was completely unavoidable.

DAVID: And what does that matter? How does that change—anything? Take all of that aside and they are still in radio silence, there was still a gun in the ceiling and there was still a goddam radio signal that—

ELI: —*I didn't hear.*
(Beat)
Okay? It wasn't that I didn't *understand* it—I didn't *hear* anything. "No Survivors"? On the transmission? It was just static. Okay? And that is *all* that I heard.
(Beat)
David?

DAVID: Yeah.

ELI: I didn't hear anything.

DAVID: Okay.

ELI: So—

DAVID: Except you told me that you did.

ELI: What I said was—

DAVID: You stood there / and you told me that. It was less than an hour ago.

ELI: And what I said was that I heard something—

DAVID: Only I'm supposed to believe you now, because now you're telling me the truth?

ELI: Yes.

DAVID: Not before, but. Now that you've decided not to lie to me because *now* you're terrified? And by the way, when the fuck are you not terrified?

ELI: Look, I didn't hear anything. Okay? It was just static and I shouldn't have lied to you, that, I can see that now—I just—I didn't want you to feel like—
(Beat)
It doesn't matter, the point is, that, I think we need to consider / the very real possibility—

DAVID: They could have seen what I was doing.

ELI: *(Beat)* I don't think that—

DAVID: They saw what I was doing, that I was going to show you and so they decided—

ELI: Yeah?

DAVID: I don't know. Maybe. Yes. They cut the transmission, or.

ELI: "No Survivors."

DAVID: Look.

ELI: In an outdated air-force code that only *you* can understand?

DAVID: *(Beat)* I get it, okay? I really do. I know what this sounds like, but I know what I heard, I know these people, and I do not intend to die waiting to see what they've got planned. So.
(Beat)
I think maybe we've been given a chance.

ELI: A chance for what?

DAVID: To hear the twig snap.

ELI: Buddy, what did I miss?

DAVID: *(Beat)* Don't worry about it.

ELI: I just—I don't see what else you were supposed to do up there. It was a—a piece of plastic that a thousand people checked over a thousand times—and you know what? It broke anyway…there was pressure that we couldn't account for, and you were *forced* to make this awful decision but that doesn't mean—

DAVID: It's done. Okay?

ELI: Wait. No.
(He begins to climb down.)

DAVID: We have a bomb now.

ELI: Please. / I am asking you to please not do this.

DAVID: I'm sorry. I'm sure you were going some place very powerful with all of that.

ELI: If you were sorry—

DAVID: Because you can't trust me. Is why I'm sorry, but I wouldn't expect you to understand that.

ELI: Because I wasn't on the secondary craft?

DAVID: No. Because you haven't ever been hunting.

ELI: I don't know / what that means.

DAVID: This is the only play that we have left.
(Beat)
All right? We're almost there.
(He walks to the COMMS system.)
(Into speaker)
Um. This is just an update. You've got less than ten minutes to open the goddam door and if you think I'm fucking around, ask Eli.

ELI: You know what?

DAVID: *(Into speaker)* So, why don't we get this over with, all right? If you can hear me, then I think you know by now that now we're both running out of time. You can see the build-up in the second, third, and seventh sectors and you can also see where what it's attached to—you know what's going on and you know what I've done. So you also know what I will do. Only I won't—if you let him go.
(Beat)
All right? Guys. He doesn't have anything to do with this. He's a college professor, he wasn't on the secondary, he doesn't know what happened which means he couldn't tell anyone even if he wanted to which he doesn't. He's a good man. He did his turn and he deserves to go home. All right? Are you listening to me? I need some indication that—

(Beat)

Here. I'm gonna back up—open the doors, you let him leave? And whatever you want to do is fine but I am telling you right now that *this* is the fucking bargain. This is how it works. So, you open the fucking doors and we can do this. All right?

(Beat. Nothing)

ELI: Maybe we should—

DAVID: *(Into speaker)* No, come on, fuckin'—somebody talk to me, here. You can see what's going on, I am telling you, this is the only option that you've got left. I do not want to do this but I will. We both know what I did. But he wasn't any part of that. He didn't do anything wrong. You have to let him go. I'm right here. I fucked up. But this is between us—

ELI: I think that…

DAVID: *(Into speaker)* I'm begging you. All right? Is that what you want to hear? I fucking—I am begging you to please, just.

(Beat)

Please.

ELI: David.

(And still. Nothing)

DAVID: *(Into speaker)* All right. You know what? Try me, then. You dumb fucks. The oxygen that we breathe comes from the exact same place and you look at the goddam build up. This is the only way that you can save *yourselves*. So do the fucking math and find out if I'm bluffing or not you *pieces of shit*.

(Beat)

ELI: Are you okay?

DAVID: *(Into speaker)* It's just that I get it; okay? I have been where you are, I have been exactly where you are right now, and if you do this...I just.
(Beat)
You can't...
(Beat)
You don't have to do this. You have time. I didn't have that, but.
(Beat)
You don't have to do this.
(Beat)
You can do it different. Differently. All right? Please.
(Beat)
Over.
(Flips a switch on the communication system. And there's a long beat.)

ELI: Listen—

DAVID: Okay, well. This is good. Um. I mean, you can't say we didn't give them a chance, right? We definitely, um, we did that and I think / that now—

ELI: Hang on.

DAVID: If anything I think that they know that we aren't fucking around, so. / They're gonna take their time, but.

ELI: Hey, slow down for a second, okay?

DAVID: I should probably go and check on the, um.

(DAVID starts walking over to his makeshift ladder, when—)

ELI: Commander?

DAVID: *(Beat)* What?

ELI: You know, I'm not entirely sure how to work in "marzipan", but.

(A light flickers.)

ELI: Look, I have no right—to ask you this, I wouldn't be here, if it wasn't for you about a thousand times, I have no right to ask you this, I know that, but. I am asking you, to just please. Please do not do this.

(It flickers again.)

ELI: I need you to give me a chance.

(It flickers again. And it goes out.)

DAVID: All right. Um. You know what? Here's what I'm gonna do. I am gonna climb up there, and when that happens my back will be turned and my hands will be full; if you want to shoot me, then that's your call, / but I would suggest that you do it then.

ELI: What are you talking about?

(DAVID puts the gun down.)

DAVID: Safety's there. It goes—like that, just. But this is the best offer I got. So.

ELI: I'm not—I can't do that.

DAVID: Yes, you can.
(Beat)
Eli? You can.
(Beat)
Okay? But. You can't say I didn't give you a chance.
(Beat)
All right?

(DAVID puts the gun in ELI's hand—and then begins straightening up.)

ELI: David.

DAVID: What?

ELI: Nothing, just. You really would have thought that getting back down on the ground would be the hard part.

DAVID: Right.

(He heads for the bomb.)

ELI: I'm not gonna shoot you. Okay? Like, you do get that, right?

DAVID: Okay.

ELI: Because the thing is that you were right. I do want the, what you said? To make a *vow*. To someone.

DAVID: Eli—

ELI: See how she's gonna...change. Every day. All the...little stuff. I wanna see that. All of it. If she will ever stop cheating at cards, only I would really like it if my friend was there with me when I do and I can't do that, if I shoot you. So. Yeah. I'm not gonna fucking do that.

(He puts down the gun.)

DAVID: Fine.

ELI: And also because I don't think you're gonna detonate this bomb. Thing.

DAVID: *(Beat)* You're wrong.

ELI: Maybe.

DAVID: You are. I think we both know / I've done worse.

ELI: Okay, but this is different.

DAVID: Why?

ELI: Because it fucking is. / It's different.

DAVID: How?

ELI: Because you didn't have a choice before.
(Beat)
Now you do.

DAVID: Really?

ELI: Yes.

DAVID: Do you see a lot of options here, Eli?

ELI: We could wait.

DAVID: Okay, but, see, *that /* is not an option. *Waiting* is not an option.

ELI: I see at least twenty-six options, not a single one of which can be solved by detonating a bomb. And a lot of these...

DAVID: What.

ELI: I dunno.
(Beat)
Could be cool.

DAVID: Okay.

ELI: I mean, space-time anomaly? Would be fucking cool. Alien abduction? If they were...nice. Maybe. Hell, heaven, limbo, purgatory. We were robots this whole time—or what if this *is* just—a COMMS system failure...thing that nobody's ever seen before—and they are out there right now, just...people, trying their best to fix it—and *failing*.

DAVID: That isn't—

ELI: Maybe a piece of plastic got...broken somewhere—inside. And. So, they didn't see it. And they can't find it. But they are trying, maybe, and, wouldn't you rather give *them* some more time? Don't you want to buy *them* all the time that you possibly can?

DAVID: I don't *want* any of this. / None of this is—

ELI: So why are you doing it, then?

DAVID: Because I can't just—

ELI: What?

DAVID: Stop it.

ELI: No, you can't just *what*?

DAVID: Sit here and do nothing while—

ELI: I'm not asking you / to do nothing.

DAVID: That is *exactly*—

ELI: I am asking you to survive.
(Beat)
Which is a lot harder.

DAVID: I can't—

ELI: Look, I don't know what's going on. I don't. If I did, I would tell you, but I don't think I can figure all that—this—out, in the next couple of minutes, and.
(Beat)
Which fucking sucks, because, just between you and me, I am terrified right now. My stomach hurts, and my hands are all…tingly, I don't know why there was a gun in the ceiling or what the clock is counting down to, *I don't know*—but I would really, really like to find out. And actually? *That* is my plan. Is to just hold on… for a little while longer and find out for myself what happens when the clock runs out. Because maybe you're right and it is…awful, maybe they are…terrible. Or maybe you're wrong. And whatever it is, it's something that we can't even…imagine yet. Maybe it's something…incredible.
(Beat)
Or maybe we're robots. I don't know, but. I would like to find that out for myself. I want to see that for myself.
(Beat)
And I think you do, too.

DAVID: Really?

ELI: Yeah, in fact I know it.

DAVID: How?

ELI: Because.

(Beat)
You're an explorer.
(Beat)
So, I'm not gonna stop you. And I'm not gonna… shoot you, I'm just.
(Beat)
What I'm gonna do is I'm gonna sit right here, and I'm gonna wait. See what happens.
(Beat)
And I would really, really like it, if my friend was—

(DAVID sits down. Right next to him. And they sit. Together. In the dark)

ELI: Thank you.

(The lights flicker violently for a moment and then they stop.)

ELI: Um. Can you still—hear it?

(DAVID nods.)

ELI: Is it pretty loud?

(DAVID nods again.)

ELI: Okay. Well, it might be, for a while. But it'll change. Eventually. It'll stop.

DAVID: How do you know?

ELI: Because everything…does. Eventually.

DAVID: Right.

ELI: Everything…changes.
(Beat)
Science.

DAVID: And how long do we…wait?

ELI: I don't know, but, probably at least until the clock runs out. See what happens.

DAVID: And then—

ELI: We try something else.

DAVID: Right.

ELI: Also science. I mean...we *do* have a bomb.

DAVID: Yeah.

ELI: Bomb's not going anywhere.

DAVID: True.

ELI: We could do all *sorts* of crazy shit.

DAVID: But we try this first, and.

ELI: Yeah.

DAVID: See what happens.

(Beat)

ELI: Right.

DAVID: Okay.

ELI: Good. We're almost there.

(Another light goes out.)

(DAVID is terrified.)

ELI: It's okay.

(But DAVID and ELI wait.)

(And breathe.)

ELI: We're okay.

(DAVID and EILI are both terrified.)

(Another light flickers.)

(And they wait.)

(And then—)

DAVID: So.
(Beat)
What's the new word?

(ELI considers.)

ELI: Um.
(Blackout)

END OF PLAY